Conestoga Wagons In Braddock's Campaign, 1755

by Don H. Berkebile

Contributions from The Museum of History and Technology: Paper 9

ISBN: 9781849027403
Cover image of Conestoga Wagon from the National Archives and Records Administration website:-
http://www.archives.gov/research/arc/

Contents

Introduction

CONESTOGA WAGONS IN BRADDOCK'S CAMPAIGN, 1755

More than 200 years have passed since the Pennsylvania farm wagon, the ancestral form of the Conestoga wagon, first won attention through military service in the French and Indian War. These early wagons, while not generally so well known, were the forerunners of the more popular Conestoga freighter of the post-Revolutionary period and also of the swaying, jolting prairie schooners that more recently carried hopeful immigrants to the western territories.

THE AUTHOR: *Don H. Berkebile is on the exhibits staff of the Smithsonian Institution's United States National Museum.*

Historical account

In a speech to the Pennsylvania Assembly on December 19, 1754, Governor Morris suggested a law that would "settle and establish the wages" to be paid for the use of the wagons and horses which soon were to be pressed into military service for the expedition against Fort DuQuesne.[1] His subsequent remarks on the subject were all too indicative of the difficulties which were later to arise. The Assembly however, neglected to pass such an act, and the Maryland and Virginia Assemblies were equally lax in making provision for General Braddock's transportation.

Sir John St. Clair had told Braddock, shortly after his arrival in the colonies in late February 1755, "of a great number of Dutch settlers, at the foot of a mountain called the Blue Ridge, who would undertake to carry by the hundred the provisions and stores...."[2] St. Clair was confident he could have 200 wagons and 1,500 pack horses at Fort Cumberland by early May. On April 21 Braddock reached Frederick, in Maryland. There he found that only 25 wagons had come in and several of these were unserviceable. Furiously the General swore that the expedition was at an end. At this point, Benjamin Franklin, who was in Frederick to placate the wrath of Braddock and St. Clair against the Pennsylvanians, commented on the advantages the expedition might have gained had it landed in Philadelphia instead Alexandria,[3] and pointed out that in eastern Pennsylvania every farmer had a wagon. Braddock then suggested that Franklin try to raise the needed 150 wagons and the 1,500 pack horses. Asking that the terms to be offered be first drawn up, Franklin agreed to the undertaking and was accordingly commissioned.

On his return to Pennsylvania, Franklin published an advertisement at Lancaster on April 26, setting forth the terms offered (the full text of this advertisement is found in Franklin's autobiography).

Although eventually successful, Franklin was beset by many difficulties in collecting the wagons. Farmers argued that they could not spare teams from the work of their farms. Others were not satisfied with the terms offered. Furthermore, the Quaker-controlled Assembly had little interest in the war and did nothing to regulate the hire of wagons, in spite of the repeated pleas of the governor. Franklin published new advertisements more strongly worded than the first, threatening an impress of wagons and drivers if better cooperation could not be had.[4] Finally the governor found it necessary to issue threatening warrants to the magistrates of four of the more reluctant counties. This action brought in the wagons but caused new difficulties to arise, for in order to prevent trouble the townships had contributed, in addition to the fifteen shillings per day offered in Franklin's terms, from five to fifteen pounds to each owner who would hire out his wagon.

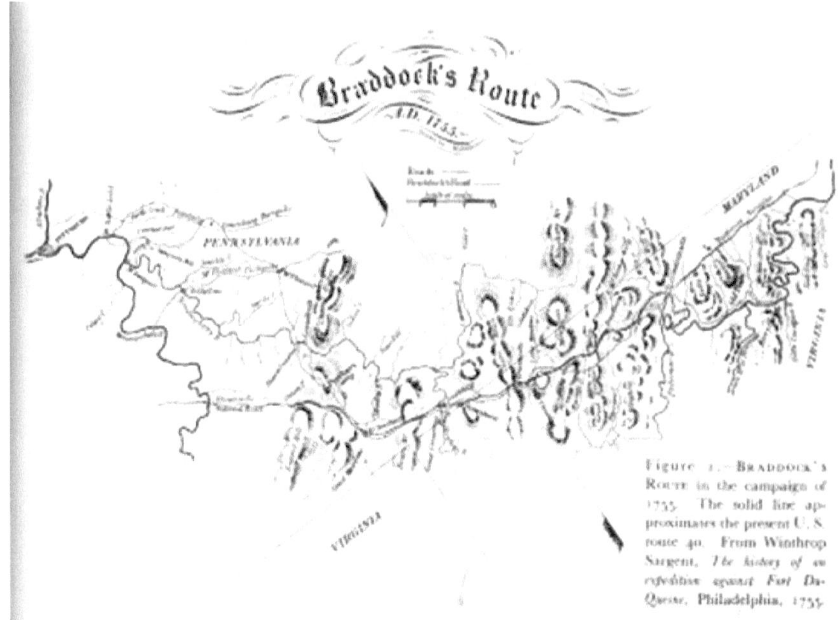

[Figure 1.—BRADDOCK'S ROUTE in the campaign of 1755. The solid line approximates the present U.S. route 40. From Winthrop Sargent, *The history of an expedition against Fort DuQuesne*, Philadelphia, 1755.]

This practice caused others to demand more for their services. Governor Morris wrote to Richard Peters that he was "preparing to send sixty waggon loads of oats and corn from hence (Philadelphia), for which I am sorry to say, that I shall be obliged to give more for the transporting of it, than the thing is worth, such advantages are taken by the people of the Public wants...."[5] Two weeks later Edward Shippen, explaining the teamsters side of the argument, told how they had to pay ferriage at the Susquehannah and make the return trip with empty wagons.[6] It would be well to mention here that not all of the wagons were to accompany the expedition; many were to transport supplies only to Conococheague[7] or to Wills Creek, and it was the owners of these wagons who, since they did not feel bound by the same terms offered the 150 accompanying the expedition, most often took advantage of the situation. In addition, wagons were needed to supply Colonel James Burd and his party, who were building the Pennsylvania road from Shippensburg to the forks of the Youghiogheny,[8] where it was to meet with Braddock's road. When word came back to the settlements that Indians had killed several of Burd's wagoners, recruiting became still more difficult. The alarm became so great that the road builders threatened to leave if protection was not sent them. Accordingly, Captain Hogg was sent with his company from Braddock's army to cover them.[9]

[Figure 2.—STRAKES BEFORE BEING COMPLETELY UNEARTHED. Strakes are sections of wagon tire, equal in number to the felloes of the wheel.]

[Figure 3.—SIX STRAKES ARRANGED IN A CIRCLE, as they would encompass a 12-spoke wheel. In the center are two extra strakes, two hub bands, and a hub boxing (the smaller ring).]

The farm wagons used in these operations were often referred to as Conestoga wagons.[10] This term was apparently in general use at least as early as 1750, when the term "Dutch Wagon" was also used in referring to this particular type of vehicle.[11] The Conestoga, deriving its name from the Conestoga valley near Lancaster, was apparently a Pennsylvania adaptation of the English wagon.[12] Unfortunately there are no existing specimens of early wagons of whose age we can be certain, and the few wagon fragments that have been unearthed are insufficient to justify any conclusions. A number of strakes[13] were found in Edmund's Swamp (figs. 2-5), on the route of the Forbes expedition in 1758. These indicate a wheel diameter of 64 inches and a tire 2 inches wide.[14] The 2-inch tires are undoubtedly relics of a farmer's wagon, since the various military vehicles had tires no less than 3 inches and often on the heavier types 4 inches wide. The use of strakes also indicates that these early wagons had no brakes such as the large Conestogas of a later era had.[15] From all indications it would appear that these early farm wagons differed from the larger freighters of the 1790's and were probably similar to the lighter, farm-type Conestogas of the 19th century. Farm wagons are somewhat smaller than road wagons, generally bear less ornamentation and lack the more graceful lines of the latter.

[Figure 4.—A STRAKE, SHOWING SPIKES. On early vehicles the tires were put on in sections and spiked in place. Later one endless tire was "sweated" on by being heated to expand it, fitted on the wheel, and cooled in place.]

[Figure 5.—BANDS AND HUB BOXING shown in figure 3. These and the strakes shown in figures 2-4, parts of an old Pennsylvania farm wagon, were found in Edmunds Swamp, Pennsylvania, along the route of the Forbes Expedition of 1758.]

Contemporary letters and newspaper advertisements attest to the fact that farm wagons were the type used by Braddock. For example, Franklin's advertisement in the *Pennsylvania Gazette* on May 22, 1755, noted that "several Neighbors may conveniently join in fitting out a Waggon, as was lately done in the Back Counties." Had these wagon owners been other than farmers of poor means, such a notation would have been unnecessary. In another communication to the inhabitants of Lancaster, York, and Cumberland Counties Franklin said, "three or four of such as cannot separately spare from the business of their Plantations a Wagon and four Horses and a Driver, may do it together, one furnishing the Waggon, another one or two Horses, and another the Driver, and divide the pay proportionably between you."[16] Many letters describe the owners of the wagons with such phrases as "the Poorer sort," and "narrow circumstances of the Country People, who are to supply the waggons...."[17] These remarks indicate that farm wagons were used and suggest that the larger Conestogas, such as were driven by professional teamsters, probably had not yet been developed.

That Braddock's wagons were small is evidenced by the loads carried. Governor Morris seems to indicate loads as small as thirty-five bushels when he sent a dispatch to Braddock informing him that he had bought "one thousand bushels of Oats and one thousand bushels of Indian Corn in this town [Philadelphia], and have directed sixty waggons to be taken up."[18] This is substantiated by a remark in Captain Orme's journal, in which he states that "The loads of all waggons were to be reduced to fourteen hundred weight...." Under the same date, June 11, he indicated that the farmers wagons were smaller than the English wagons when he wrote "all the King's waggons were also sent back to the fort, they being too heavy and requiring large horses for the shafts...."[19] Another communication from Morris states that he "dispatched fifty-two waggons from this town, each carrying fifty bushels of grain, one half oats the ether Indian Corn."[20] This makes a load of about 2,200 pounds,[21] quite in agreement with the statement in the *Gentlemen's Magazine* of August 1755, that loads were commonly around one ton. A load of one ton is small in comparison to those hauled by later wagons that sometimes carried as much as five or even six tons.

An approximate description of the size of the wagon, taken from the earliest existing specimens of the same type shows a bed about 12 feet long on the bottom and 14 feet on the top. Depth of the bed ran about 32 inches and the width was approximately 42 to 46 inches. Though there was little standardization in most features, eight bows usually supported the dull white homespun cover. The diameter of the front wheels varied from 40 to 45 inches, while the rear wheels ran 10 to 20 inches larger.[22]

[Figure 6.—RESTORED FREIGHT-CARRYING CONESTOGA WAGON, about 1830, in the collection of the author. The tongue is not full length. (*Photo by the author.*)]

For a 1759 expedition it was recommended that wagon accessories include drag chains, grass cutting knives, axes, shovels, tar buckets (for lubricating axles), jacks, hobbles, and extra sets of such items as clouts (axle-bearing plates), nails, horseshoes, hames, linch pins, and hamestrings.[23] It is doubtful if many teamsters in the 1755 expedition had so complete a selection of equipment; campaign experience in the mountains of western Pennsylvania was necessary to convince them of this necessity. There is no evidence that the hame bells later to be found on professional teams were used at this early date. The advertisement[24] that was circulated for the 1759 expedition mentions a "slip bell ... for each horse" among the items necessary on an expedition, so it is possible that some drivers of the 1755 expedition may have used a single bell on each horse, as was the custom with pack horses. These bells, kept stuffed during the day, were unstuffed at night when the horses were put out to forage in the woods so that they might be more easily found in the morning. Orme mentions no bells, although he writes of other methods used to avoid losing horses at night.

Early in May detachments of the Army began to arrive at Wills Creek. During the advance to Wills Creek the lack of transportation had been keenly felt. Wagons had been forced to shuttle back and forth between camps in order to keep all stores and provisions moving forward.[25] By the latter part of May the Pennsylvania wagons were coming in; about 90 arrived on May 20. That same night 30 wagons had to be sent on to Winchester to bring up to Wills Creek the provisions which could not be brought earlier for lack of wagons. Also, 300 of the pack horses had to be sent back to Conococheague, through which the wagons had just passed, to bring up the flour which agent Cresap of that place had through neglect or intention failed to forward in the wagons as he had been directed. On May 27, 100 wagons were on hand, with some still coming in.[26] According to the accounts of the commission later appointed to settle wagoner's claims, 146 wagons with teams, and about 510 pack horses were provided by Pennsylvanians to accompany the army.[27]

[Figure 7.—FARM-TYPE CONESTOGA WAGON, about 1850 in the collection of the author. The tongue is not full length. (*Photo by the author.*)]

As the army prepared to move from Fort Cumberland, William Shirley, secretary to General Braddock, advised Governor Morris "we move from this place with 200 Waggons."[28] In many communications such as this there appears a certain looseness in reporting numbers in round figures, and also in using the words "waggons" or "carriages" in an all inclusive sense. It is obvious that such figures must often have included any wheeled vehicle, and sometimes even the gun carriages. Thus the figure 200 undoubtedly includes 145 Pennsylvania wagons,[29] plus a number of British Army wagons, tumbrils, and perhaps gun carriages. By Braddock's own count he had about 40 wagons over and above those he got from Pennsylvania;[30] how many of these were British wagons, tumbrils, or possibly a few of the wagons Gage had impressed on his march to Wills Creek, is unknown.[31]

From the beginning of the march, the roads were a challenge, for both Braddock's and Burd's roads presented what appeared to be unsurmountable obstacles. An examination of the terrain over which they had to pass causes far greater respect for these road builders and drivers than is usually accorded them. Orme again comes forward with the picture of their labors. Major Chapman had marched from Wills Creek at daybreak of May 30,[32] with the advance unit of the army and, says Orme, "it was night before the whole baggage had got over a mountain about two miles from the camp. The ascent and descent were almost a perpendicular rock; three waggons were entirely destroyed, which were replaced from the camp; and many more were extremely shattered."[33] Braddock went out from the fort and reconnoitered this section of road. Although 300 men and the company of miners had been working on the road for several days, the General "thought it impassable by howitzers," and was about to put another 300 to work when Lt. Spendelowe of the detachment of seamen informed him of an easier route he had found.[34] Thus the remainder of the wagons were spared the trip over the "perpendicular rock."

In addition to these difficulties of baggage movement, there was the unavoidable peril of losing horses, particularly at night. Orme gives the following description of the situation:[35]

> Most of the horses which brought up the train were either lost, or carried home by their owners, the nature of the country making it impossible to avoid this fatal inconvenience, the whole being a continual forest for several hundred miles without inclosures or bounds by which horses can be secured: they must be turned into the woods for their subsistance, and feed upon leaves and young shoots of trees. Many projects, such as belts, hobles, &c., were tried, but none of these were a security against the wildness of the country and the knavery of the people we were obliged to employ: by these means we lost our horses almost as fast as we could collect them, and those which remained grew very weak, so we found ourselves every day less able to undertake the extra-ordinary march we were to perform.

Braddock soon appointed a Wagon Master General, and under him wagon masters, horse masters, and drovers. By his order, horses were to be mustered both morning and evening. When the men made camp, the wagons were to be drawn up in a single line along the road, with an interval between companies. The horses were then turned into the woods to feed, surrounded by a line of sentinels who were not to permit any horses to pass them.

By June 16, when the first brigade reached Little Meadows, Braddock realized that the advance of his column was being retarded and his troops weakened by the number of wagons in his train.[36] Washington, who had profited from his 1754 experiences in Pennsylvania, previously had recommended that Braddock use more pack horses and fewer wagons.[37] It became obvious that wagons, while ordinarily superior to pack animals, lost this advantage if the roads were not sufficiently opened to admit their easy passage. In view of this, Braddock decided to advance from Little Meadows with a picked detachment of 1,300 men and a minimum of wagons, about 30 in number, and to leave the heavier baggage with 84 wagons in charge of Colonel Dunbar and his 850 men.[38] Prior to this re-organization at Little Meadows, four horse teams had been used in accordance with the terms of Franklin's advertisements. Now, however, the advance unit of the army marched with six horses to a wagon,[39] a change necessitated equally by the rugged terrain and the hastily constructed roads with which they were forced to contend, and by the poor condition of the horses.[40]

While this lightened column moved forward more rapidly, the mountainous and rocky roads continued to impede the progress of the army. On the morning of June 25 so steep a grade was encountered that the men were obliged to ease the carriages down with tackles. Throughout the remainder of June and the early part of July the column was so retarded by the road conditions that only a few miles could be covered each day.[41] By July 4 the country had become less difficult and the army was able to add a few more miles to the daily march. At one o'clock on the afternoon of July 9 this small train of wagons moved over the second ford of the Monongahela between the troops of the 44th and 48th regiments. A short time later the unfortunate expedition met defeat for all its efforts. As the battle drew to a close, many of the surviving troops began to gather around the wagons. This drew heavier fire on the wagons and at this point, said Franklin, "the waggoners took each a horse out of his team and scamper'd."[42]

As evening drew on, the wounded Braddock sent Washington back to Dunbar's Camp, nearly 45 miles behind, to order wagons forward with provisions and hospital stores and to transport the wounded back to Wills Creek. A number of these wagons met the retreating army on July 11, at Gist's Plantation; then, after wounds were dressed, they returned to Dunbar's Camp. There most of the wagons were gathered with the stores and burned in order to keep them from the hands of the enemy. The survivors continued their retreat, accompanied by a few of the wagons loaded with wounded comrades.

The number of Pennsylvania wagons that arrived back at Wills Creek has not been definitely established. For the service of their wagons, 30 owners received payment for a period greater than the 51 days, but of these, only 10 were paid for services beyond what appears to be July 20.[43] Only the wagon of William Douglas, out of 146 wagons involved, seems to have survived the campaign intact.[44] Inasmuch as the other owners were reimbursed for the loss of their wagons, it is likely that those few that arrived back at Fort Cumberland were so badly damaged as to render them unserviceable, and therefore not worth driving back to eastern Pennsylvania.

Seven criticisms were made of Braddock's advance to the forks of the Ohio. Of these seven, six, in varying degrees, concern transportation.[45] In choosing Alexandria to land his troops he put himself more distant from the needed wagons; his horses were too few and too weak to bear the burden of all the supplies on the entire march, without depots having first been established at the various camps along the line of march; his troops were delayed by the progress of the wagons and by the necessity of their having to help with the wagons; the roads were inadequate in many places for the excessively heavy artillery and the wagons; the pack horses were weakened by the extra service they were required to perform; and due to his lack of horses, Dunbar had been left too far behind.[46] While other factors contributed to the outcome of the expedition, many of the officers learned, as had Washington in 1754, the importance of proper transportation.

The Conestoga Wagon and the Prairie Schooner

Styles in farm equipment change slowly, and it is probable that the farm-type Conestoga wagon of about 1850 shown in figure 7 is similar in many respects to the Pennsylvania wagons used by Braddock a century earlier. The prairie schooner, too, bore many of the characteristics of these early farm wagons. It was about the same length as the Conestoga wagon, but the lines of the bed were straight rather than curved and the bows supporting the cloth cover were upright rather than slanting fore and aft. Also, the prairie schooner had a seat where the driver, or at least his family, could ride during the seemingly endless days of the journey.

In this respect the prairie schooner differed not only from the early farm wagons, but also from the large freighting Conestogas, like that in figure 6, which dates from about 1830. In the years following the Revolution and before the coming of the railroad these freighters were used to carry all types of merchandise to Pittsburgh from Philadelphia by way of present route U.S. 30 and from Baltimore by way of present route U.S. 40.

The freighting Conestoga had no inside seats, and the teamster, when not walking by his team, either rode the left wheel horse or the "lazy board" projecting from the left side of the wagon, just in front of the rear wheel. It is distinguished by its distinctive, overhanging end bows, from which swept down the characteristic homespun cover, and by its lines, which are longer and more graceful than those of either the later prairie schooner or the earlier Pennsylvania farm wagon.

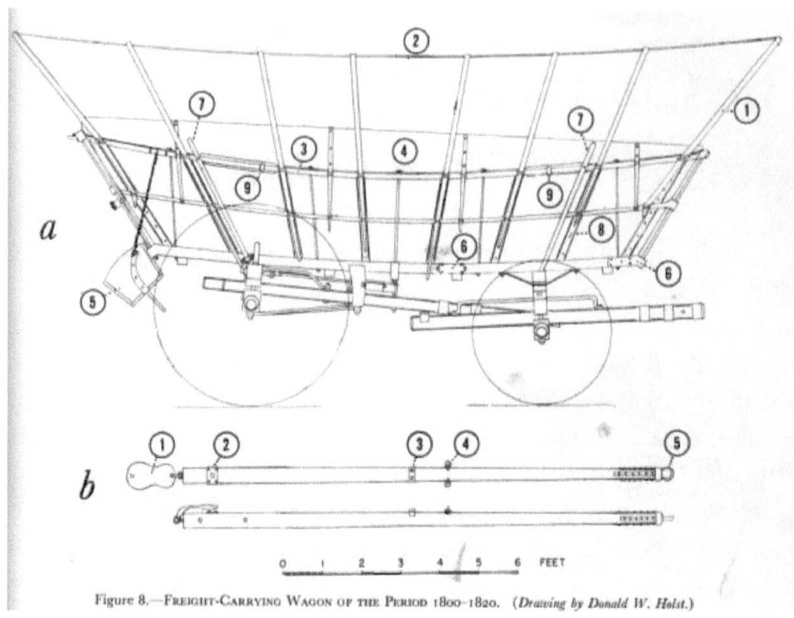

Figure 8.—FREIGHT-CARRYING WAGON OF THE PERIOD 1800-1820. (*Drawing by Donald W. Holst.*)]

This drawing and those of figures 9 and 10 are from specifications, sketches, and photographs, now in the files of the division of transportation, U.S. National Museum, taken in 1925 by Paul E. Garber from a wagon then the property of Amos Gingrich, Lancaster, Pennsylvania. This wagon is illustrated in John Omwake's *Conestoga six-horse bell teams*, 1750-1850, Cincinnati, 1930, pp. 57, 63, 87.

a: Bed and running gear, right side: 1, Bows for supporting cover. 2, Ridgepole, or stringer. 3, Top rail, with bow staples and side-board staples. 4, Side-boards, removable. 5, Feedbox in traveling position. 6, Rubbing plates to prevent wheels wearing wooden frame. 7, Side-board standards, forming framework of sides (on the inside, a few of these sometimes project a few inches above the top rail to support the side-boards). 9, Securing rings for the ends of the spread chains, two of which span the bed to give extra support to the sides against inside pressures.

b: Tongue, or pole, top and side views: 1, doubletree hasp, shown in proper position over the doubletree in the lower drawing: the hammer-headed doubletree pin goes through it, then through the doubletree and the tongue. 2, Wear plate for doubletree pin. 3, Feedbox staple; in use, the feedbox is unhooked from the rear, the long pin on one end of the box is passed through the hole for the doubletree pin, and the lug on the other end of the box is slipped through the staple. 4, Hitching rings, for securing horses while feeding. 5, End ring.

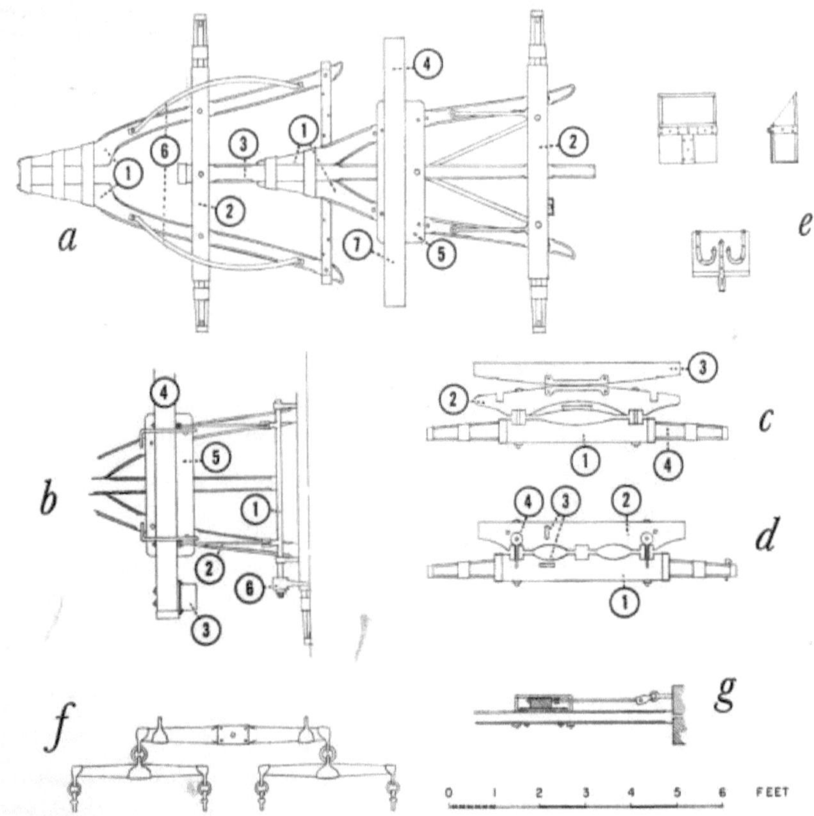

Figure 9.—Details of the Freight-Carrying Wagon, 1800–1820, of Figure 8. (*Drawing by Donald W. Holst.*)

[Figure 9.—DETAILS OF THE FREIGHT-CARRYING WAGON, 1800-1820, OF FIGURE 8. (*Drawing by Donald W. Holst.*)]

a: Running gear, top view: 1, Front and rear hounds. 2, Bolsters, with axletrees directly underneath. 3, Coupling pole. 4, Brake beam. 5, Brake-beam shelf, or support. 6, Segments forming the fifth wheel; these prevented the bed from toppling, or swaying excessively on turns. 7, Rear brace for front hounds, to keep tongue from dropping.

b: Brake mechanism, detail: 1, Brake rocker bar, with squared end for brake lever. 2, Rods connecting rocker bar to brake beam. 3, Rubber, or brakeshoe, made of wood, often faced with old leather. 4, Brake beam. 5, Brake-beam shelf, or support. 6, Brake lever, often 4 or 5 feet long.

c: Front axletree and bolsters, front view: 1, Axletree. 2, Bolster, showing wear plates. 3, Upper bolster, actually part of the wagon bed. 4, Axle, showing ironing.

d: Rear axletree and bolster, rear view: 1, Axle tree, showing linchpin in position in right axle. 2, Bolster. 3, Hook and staple for holding bucket of tar used in lubricating axles. 4, Hound pins.

e: Toolbox, showing front, end, and top; it was secured to left side of wagon.

f: Doubletree, with singletrees attached.

g: Brake mechanism, side view.

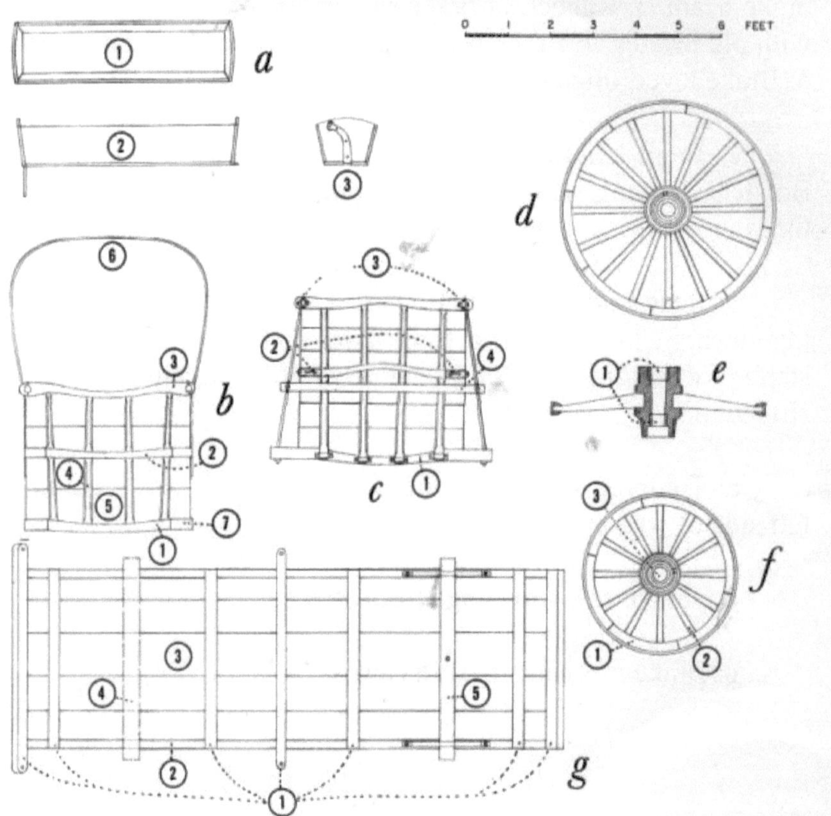

Figure 10.—DETAILS OF THE FREIGHT-CARRYING WAGON, 1800–1820, OF FIGURE 8. (*Drawing by Donald W. Holst.*)

Figure 10.—DETAILS OF THE FREIGHT-CARRYING WAGON, 1800-1820, OF FIGURE 8. (*Drawing by Donald W. Holst.*)

a: Feedbox: 1, Top. 2, Side, showing pin and lug for securing to tongue. 3, End, showing bracket into which the chains hooked for traveling.

b: Front end panel: 1, Bottom end rail. 2, Middle end rail. 3, Top end rail. 4, Standard, or upright, forming end framing. 5, End boards. 6, Bow. 7, Corner plates.

c: Rear end gate: 1, Staples for end-gate standards. 2, End-gate hasps and hooks. 3, Pins to secure gate to upper side rails. 4, Crossbar to give extra support to end gate.

d: Rear wheel.

e: Cross section of wheel: 1, Boxings, of cast iron, wedged in hub to take wear of axle.

f: Front wheel: 1, Felly, or felloe. 2, Spoke. 3, Hub, or nave.

g: Floor of wagon, from under side: 1, Crossbeams, the center and rear ones being heavier, and projecting at the ends to hold the iron side braces visible in figure 8,*a*. 2, Bottom side rails. 3, Floorboards. 4, Position of rear bolster when bed is on running gear. 5, Front bolster, showing hole for kingpin.

Footnotes

[1] *Pennsylvania Archives*, ser. 8, vol. 5, Morris to the House, Dec. 19, 1754.

[2] Robert Orme's Journal, *in* Winthrop Sargent, *The history of an expedition against Fort DuQuesne*, p. 288, Philadelphia, 1855.

[3] Benjamin Franklin, *Autobiography*, p. 166, New York, 1939.

[4] *Pennsylvania Archives*, ser. 1, vol. 2, pp. 295-96. Franklin suggested that St. Clair, with a body of troops, would probably enter Pennsylvania and take what he wanted, if it could not be obtained otherwise.

[5] *Ibid.*, ser. 1, vol. 2, Morris to Peters, May 30, 1755.

[6] *Ibid.*, Shippen to Morris, June 13, 1755.

[7] The modern spelling is given above. A number of spellings were common in 1755, among them Conegogee, Connecochieg, and Cannokagig.

[8] This is the modern spelling. Among those used in 1755 were Yoxhio Geni and Ohiogany.

[9] *Pennsylvania Archives*, ser. 1, vol. 2, Shippen to Allen, June 30, 1755. Also, Orme's Journal, in Sargent, *op. cit.* (footnote 2) p. 329.

[10] Originally spelled Conestogoe. The first known reference to a Conestoga wagon appears under date of 1717 in James Logan's "Account Book, 1712-1719," the manuscript original of which is in the Historical Society of Pennsylvania, in Philadelphia. It is likely that the

reference was only to a wagon from Conestogoe, and not to a definite type of vehicle.

[11] The term seems to have been in common use by 1750 since a tavern in Philadelphia, called "The Sign of the Conestogoe Waggon," was mentioned in an advertisement in the *Pennsylvania Gazette*, February 5, 1750, but another advertisement, (*ibid.*, February 12, 1750), in referring to what was apparently the same establishment, uses the term "Dutch Waggon."

[12] It is not certain at this time whether English or German styles influenced the Conestoga wagon most. Judging from some early English wagons still in existence, it would appear that some of these lines were followed. Even today some farmers, and those who have been close to the wagon and its use, frequently refer to the Conestoga type as "English wagons."

[13] Strakes are sections of wagon tire, equal in number to the felloes of a wheel. On early vehicles the tires were put on in sections and spiked in place. Later, one endless tire was "sweated" on, by being heated, fitted on the wheel, and cooled in place.

[14] Found in 1953 by the Field Corps for Historical Research, these strakes are obviously from rear wheels. Though dimensions were by no means standardized, front wheels were always smaller, so that in turning the wagon the tires would be less likely to rub the sides of the wagon box.

[15] Strakes were spiked onto the wheel with large square headed nails, as indicated in figure 3, and a brake shoe would have been rapidly torn to pieces by rubbing against them.

[16] *Pennsylvania Archives*, ser. 1, vol. 2, pp. 295-96.

[17] *Ibid.*, ser. 1, vol. 2, Shippen to Morris, February 17, 1756; and ser. 4, vol. 2, Denny to Amherst, March 3, 1759.

[18] *Ibid.*, ser. 1, vol. 2, Morris to Braddock, June 4, 1755.

[19] Orme's Journal, in Sargent, *op. cit.* (footnote 2), pp. 331-32. English wagons were equipped with pairs of shafts, similar to those of a spring wagon or buggy of recent times. Wagon shafts were, however, much heavier than the latter.

[20] *Pennsylvania Archives*, ser. 4, vol. 2, Morris to Braddock, June 12, 1755.

[21] R. Moore, *The universal assistant*, p. 205, New York, n. d. The weight of corn is given at 56 pounds per bushel, and oats at 32 pounds per bushel.

[22] One light wagon of about 1800 had smaller wheels, the front being 37 inches and the rear 49 inches in diameter.

[23] *Pennsylvania Archives*, ser. 1, vol. 3, advertisement of General Stanwix for wagons, May 4, 1759.

[24] *Ibid.*

[25] Will H. Lowdermilk, *Edward Braddock's orderly books*, Cumberland, 1880, p. 25.

[26] Seaman's Journal, in Sargent, *op. cit.* (footnote 2), p. 380.

[27] Lewis Burd Walker, ed., *The settlement of the waggoners' accounts*, 1899.

[28] *Pennsylvania Archives*, ser. 1, vol. 2, Shirley to Morris, June 7, 1755.

[29] Walker, *op. cit.* (footnote 27), p. 20. Of the 146 wagons, one was apparently unserviceable by the time it reached Wills Creek. Its owner was paid only for his services and the use of his team.

[30] Orme's Journal, in Sargent, *op. cit.* (footnote 2), p. 321.

[31] *Ibid.*, p. 312.

[32] *Ibid.*, p. 323. There is some question here whether the incident reported occurred near Wills Creek, or on June 15 in the Allegheny Mountains. Orme reports two such incidents with identical figures and nearly identical language. Perhaps he was confusing the two places.

[33] *Ibid.*, p. 334. When wagons were damaged on the march, and repair was impossible, the load was divided among the other wagons and the unserviceable wagon abandoned.

[34] *Ibid.*, p. 324 (see also Seaman's Journal, in Sargent, *op. cit.* (footnote 2), p. 381). A detachment of 30 seamen and several officers had been detached from the fleet and assigned to the expedition to offer assistance in rigging cordages, in the event that the erection of bridges would be necessary.

[35] *Ibid.*, p. 313.

[36] *Ibid.*, p. 334 (see also Seaman's Journal, in Sargent, *op. cit.* (footnote 2), p. 383). At times it was necessary for half the troops to ground their arms and assist in moving the wagons up or down grades.

[37] Douglas S. Freeman, *George Washington*, vol. 1, p. 140, New York, 1949. Washington had written his brother John on June 14 and given his opinion that they should "retrench the wagons and increase the number of bat horses."

[38] Sargent, *op. cit.* (footnote 2), p. 203. Wagons apparently carried only artillery stores and other ammunition with the advance detachment. All provisions were carried on pack horses.

[39] Orme's Journal, in Sargent, *op. cit.* (footnote 2), p. 336.

[40] *Ibid.*, p. 332. Orme said the condition of the army was such that they could not reject any horses, a situation that was used to advantage by many contractors. He refers to the horses as "The offcasts of Indian traders, and scarce able to stand under one hundred weight." By contract they were to have carried twice that load.

[41] *Ibid.*, pp. 342-346. On June 26, due to the "extreme badness of the road," the army covered 4 miles; on June 27, 6 miles; June 28, 5 miles;

and on June 30 passage over a mountain reduced the day's march to 2 miles.

[42] Walker, *op. cit.* (footnote 27). It is interesting to note in the Waggoners' Accounts which of the teamsters apparently took a horse and "scamper'd." On the accounts of a number of them is entered the remark "to a horse returned," indicating that they were first credited for the loss of wagon and team, but the value of one horse was deducted in the final settlement, the one horse having arrived safely back at Wills Creek, in company, no doubt, with its anxious driver.

[43] A true picture is not presented here, since the accounts, except for a few cases, do not contain either the number of days for which the owners were paid or the dates of service. Only the amounts paid are given, which, if broken down at 15 shillings per day, at first would appear to indicate the last date of service. However, since it is not known which, if any, of these wagons went to Winchester before the march, no accurate conclusions can be reached. There can be little doubt that the few wagons that reached Wills Creek late in July were among the 30.

[44] Walker, *op. cit.* (footnote 27), p. 24. Douglas was not reimbursed for the loss of his wagon and was paid for an additional 55 days of service at a slightly reduced rate, due to the loss of one horse.

[45] Freeman, *op. cit.* (footnote 37), vol. 2, p. 89.

[46] *Ibid.*, p. 90. As wagons had been shuttled back in April, it was also necessary for Dunbar to shuttle horses, drawing up the first of his wagons one day and returning with his few horses on the following day to bring up the balance of the wagons.

U.S. GOVERNMENT PRINTING OFFICE: 1959

Also from Benediction Books ...

Wandering Between Two Worlds: Essays on Faith and Art
Anita Mathias
Benediction Books, 2007
152 pages
ISBN: 0955373700

Available from www.amazon.com, www.amazon.co.uk

In these wide-ranging lyrical essays, Anita Mathias writes, in lush, lovely prose, of her naughty Catholic childhood in Jamshedpur, India; her large, eccentric family in Mangalore, a sea-coast town converted by the Portuguese in the sixteenth century; her rebellion and atheism as a teenager in her Himalayan boarding school, run by German missionary nuns, St. Mary's Convent, Nainital; and her abrupt religious conversion after which she entered Mother Teresa's convent in Calcutta as a novice. Later rich, elegant essays explore the dualities of her life as a writer, mother, and Christian in the United States--Domesticity and Art, Writing and Prayer, and the experience of being "an alien and stranger" as an immigrant in America, sensing the need for roots.

About the Author

Anita Mathias was born in India, has a B.A. and M.A. in English from Somerville College, Oxford University and an M.A. in Creative Writing from the Ohio State University. Her essays have been published in The Washington Post, The London Magazine, The Virginia Quarterly Review, Commonweal, Notre Dame Magazine, America, The Christian Century, Religion Online, The Southwest Review, Contemporary Literary Criticism, New Letters, The Journal, and two of HarperSanFrancisco's The Best Spiritual Writing anthologies. Her non-fiction has won fellowships from The National Endowment for the Arts; The Minnesota State Arts Board; The Jerome Foundation, The Vermont Studio Center; The Virginia Centre for the Creative Arts, and the First Prize for the Best General Interest Article from the Catholic Press Association of the United States and Canada. Anita has taught Creative Writing at the College of William and Mary, and now lives and writes in Oxford, England.

www.anitamathias.com,
christiancogitations.blogspot.com
wanderingbetweentwoworlds.blogspot.com

www.ingramcontent.com/pod-product-compliance
Ingram Content Group UK Ltd.
Pitfield, Milton Keynes, MK11 3LW, UK
UKHW041903190726
13854UKWH00003B/1067

9 781849 027403